Income the Easy Way: Stress-Free Earning from Home

Table of Contents

1. **Introduction**
   - Welcome to Stress-Free Earning: Why Working from Home Is the Dream
   - Defining "Easy" Income: Separating Myths from Reality

2. **The Mindset for Success**
   - Escape the 9-to-5 Mental Shackles: Your New Way of Thinking
   - How to Stay Motivated When Your Office Is Also Your Couch

3. **Exploring Your Options (With Real-Life Stories!)**
   - Freelancing: From Hobbyist to Paid Expert
   - E-Commerce: How Selling Your Hobby Can Fund Your Vacation

- Passive Income: Money While You Sleep (Literally)

4. **Tools You Actually Need**
   - The Tech Essentials for Home Success
   - Free (or Nearly Free) Apps That Make Work Easier

5. **Finding Your Perfect Path (Without Guessing)**
   - The "Skills and Thrills" Test
   - Example Pathways Based on Interests

6. **The Step-by-Step Playbook**
   - Setting Up Your Home Base
   - Building an Audience (Even If You Hate Social Media)
   - Getting Paid Without Stress

7. **Scaling Up Without Losing Your Chill**
   - Turning One Client Into Ten
   - Automating the Boring Stuff

8. **Real-Life Success Stories**
   - "The Accidental Blogger" Who Earned $50,000 in a Year
   - How One Mom Funded Her Kid's College with Digital Products

9. **The Endgame: Building Lasting Wealth**
    - From Side Hustle to Full-Time Freedom
    - Your Long-Term Plan

Chapter 1: Introduction

Welcome to Stress-Free Earning: Why Working from Home Is the Dream

Imagine this : It's a Tuesday morning, but not just any Tuesday. While your neighbor wrestles with an ill-tempered alarm clock and gulps down lukewarm coffee in a rush, you're still in your pajamas, savoring the rich aroma of your favorite brew. The soundtrack to your morning isn't the blaring honk of traffic but the soft hum of your favorite playlist. Your "commute" is a leisurely stroll to the kitchen, maybe detouring to the couch for a cuddle with your dog.

Your office? It could be the spare room you converted into a cozy workspace or simply your dining table with a laptop. The best part? You're in charge. You set the hours. You decide what to wear (or not wear). Your boss is you.

Sounds like a fantasy, doesn't it? It's not. This is the reality for millions of people who've discovered the freedom of earning from home. And spoiler alert: this could be your reality too.

Why Home-Based Income is the Future

A few decades ago, working from home might have meant stuffing envelopes or answering the phone for late-night TV ads. Today, it means creating digital products, freelancing, teaching online, or even building an empire on social media. The possibilities are endless, and they're growing every day.

Why? Because the world has shifted. Remote work, side hustles, and online businesses aren't just trends—they're the new normal. People are ditching rigid schedules and office politics for a life that prioritizes flexibility, autonomy, and, let's be honest, way more time in sweatpants.

Working from home doesn't just mean avoiding traffic (though that's a perk we'd all love). It means reclaiming your time, living on your terms, and maybe even sneaking in a midday nap — because you can.

The Reality Check: What "Easy" Income Really Means

Now, before you start picturing yourself sipping margaritas on a tropical beach while your bank account magically fills up, let's set the record straight. "Easy" income doesn't mean "effort-free" income. This isn't some cheesy late-night infomercial promising millions for doing absolutely nothing.

What it does mean is working smarter, not harder. It's about building systems that let you earn without constantly trading your time for money. Think of it like planting a garden: you put in some effort upfront, water the seeds, and watch as they grow and bloom into something amazing.

Let's break it down with some examples to make it real:

Example 1: Sarah's Freelancing Journey

Sarah was always good at writing. She had a knack for words and a love for storytelling, but she'd never considered it a "real" skill. After losing her 9-to-5 job during a wave of layoffs, a friend suggested she try freelancing. At first, Sarah was skeptical—who would pay her to write?

She created a profile on Fiverr, a popular freelancing platform, and offered to write blog posts for small businesses. To her surprise, she got her first client within a week! Fast forward six months, and Sarah now has steady work, charging $100 per blog post. She picks her projects, works when it suits her, and earns more than she ever did in her corporate job.

The best part? Her mornings start with yoga instead of a commute, and her afternoons often include a walk with her dog. Her biggest challenge? Deciding whether to work from her desk or the hammock in her backyard.

Example 2: Jake's Passive Income Success

Jake is a graphic designer with a talent for creating sleek, minimalist logos. One day, he stumbled upon Creative Market, a platform where designers sell digital products like templates, fonts, and graphics.

Jake decided to try it out. He spent a weekend designing 10 logo templates and uploaded them to the platform. Within a week, he made his first sale. Over the next year, those same 10 templates earned Jake $8,000 in passive income.

What makes this story even sweeter? Jake didn't have to do any extra work after the initial upload. Every sale happened while he was doing other things—like binge-watching his favorite series or hanging out with friends.

Example 3: Lisa's E-Commerce Adventure

Lisa loved crafting—specifically, making handmade candles. Her friends often raved about how amazing they smelled and looked. One day, a friend joked, "You could sell these!"

Lisa decided to give it a shot. She set up an Etsy shop and posted pictures of her candles. Within the first month, she had orders from all over the country. Soon, Lisa was earning enough to cover her car payment—just by doing something she loved.

Why "Easy" is Achievable for You

The secret to earning from home isn't about luck or being some kind of super genius. It's about tapping into what you're already good at, using tools and platforms that make the process smoother, and taking small, consistent steps toward your goal.

Let's talk about tools for a second. The internet is your playground:

- Platforms like Fiverr and Upwork connect freelancers with clients.
- Shopify and Etsy make selling products online a breeze.
- Tools like Canva and Zoom simplify design and communication.

These platforms handle the heavy lifting—things like payments, marketing, and customer management—so you can focus on what you do best.

Why Start Now?

Here's a little secret: the best time to start was yesterday. The second-best time? Right now. The internet is a goldmine of opportunities, and every day you wait is a day someone else gets ahead.

But don't worry—it's not a race. It's a journey, and this book is your guide. Whether you want to earn an extra $500 a month or replace your full-time income, you'll find everything you need to get started in the chapters ahead.

So grab that coffee (or tea), get comfortable, and let's turn your dreams of stress-free income into a reality. The possibilities are endless, and the best part? You're about to discover them all. Ready to dive in? Let's do this!

Chapter 2: The Mindset for Success
Escape the 9-to-5 Mental Shackles: Your New Way of Thinking

Picture this: You're standing in line at Blockbuster, holding a VHS tape of the latest blockbuster (pun intended). It's 1998, and you can't wait to get home, microwave some popcorn, and watch your movie. Fast-forward 20 years, and the idea of renting a VHS sounds downright prehistoric. That's because we've all moved on to Netflix, Hulu, and YouTube — a new way of consuming entertainment that's faster, smarter, and infinitely more flexible.

The same shift is happening in the world of work. The traditional 9-to-5 job is the Blockbuster of today—structured, outdated, and full of limitations. Working from home is the Netflix of the career world: adaptable, modern, and tailored to your life.

But to truly succeed in this new world, you need to rewire the way you think about work. Forget hourly paychecks and rigid schedules. Your focus should be on creating value. That's what people will pay for.

Example: Mary the Pet Portrait Artist

Mary always thought her love of drawing was just a quirky talent. She spent her evenings sketching cartoons and doodling while watching TV. It never crossed her mind that people would pay for her work—until a friend suggested she try selling custom pet portraits on Etsy.

Mary decided to give it a shot. She created a few sample drawings, set up a shop, and started sharing her work on social media. Within a week, she had her first order—a portrait of a golden retriever named Max. By the end of her first month, she'd earned $1,200.

What changed for Mary? She stopped treating her talent as a hobby and started treating it as a valuable service. She realized that people weren't just paying for a drawing; they were paying for a unique keepsake of their beloved pets.

Why This Matters

The lesson here is simple: you are more valuable than you think. Whether you're a great cook, a skilled typist, or a talented photographer, your skills have worth. The key is understanding how to package them into something people want.

So, ask yourself:

- What am I good at?
- What do people compliment me on?
- How can I turn that into something people will pay for?

How to Stay Motivated When Your Office Is Also Your Couch

Let's face it: working from home has its perks, but it also has its challenges. Sure, you get to avoid office politics and awkward watercooler conversations, but you also face a new enemy—your couch.

The line between "work" and "relaxation" can blur when your home becomes your office. Without a boss looking over your shoulder, it's easy to slip into a Netflix binge or decide that today is a great day to reorganize your pantry instead of answering emails.

The trick? Treat your home-based work like it's a "real" job.

Rituals to Stay Productive

Begin your day with a routine that signals, "It's time to work." Maybe it's making a cup of coffee, meditating for five minutes, or writing down your to-do list. The goal is to create a mental shift from "home mode" to "work mode."

Create a dedicated workspace — even if it's just a corner of your dining table. Avoid working from your bed or the couch, as it blurs the line between relaxation and productivity.

Use a timer to structure your work hours. For example, work for 50 minutes and then take a 10-minute break. Apps like Focus Booster or Pomodoro Tracker can help you stay disciplined.

Example: Jason the Freelance Writer

Jason is a freelance writer who works from a tiny studio apartment. At first, he struggled to stay productive—his bed was always calling his name, and his TV was just a click away. Then Jason discovered the power of rituals.

Every morning, he starts his day by lighting a candle that smells like the ocean. For Jason, this simple act signals the beginning of his "workday." He also sets a timer to work in 45-minute bursts, followed by 15-minute breaks where he stretches, makes tea, or scrolls through Instagram guilt-free.

This small change transformed Jason's productivity. His mornings became focused, his afternoons productive, and his evenings guilt-free because he knew he had accomplished his goals for the day.

Why Rituals Work

Rituals are powerful because they create structure and consistency. When you work from home, it's easy to lose track of time or let distractions take over. Rituals give you control, helping you switch into "work mode" and stay there.

- Dress the Part: Even if you're working from home, getting out of pajamas and into casual clothes can shift your mindset.
- Reward Yourself: Finish a big task? Treat yourself to a fancy coffee or 20 minutes of your favorite TV show.
- Track Your Wins: At the end of each day, write down three things you accomplished. This keeps you motivated and reminds you of your progress.

The Big Takeaway

Success from home starts with the right mindset. Escape the trap of thinking about work in traditional terms—hourly paychecks, rigid schedules, and the constant grind. Instead, focus on creating value and building rituals that keep you productive and inspired.

And remember: the freedom to work from home is a gift, but it's also a responsibility. Use it wisely, and you'll not only earn an income but create a life you truly love.

Now, let's move on to the fun part—exploring the different ways you can start earning from home! Get ready to turn your skills, hobbies, and passions into serious cash.

Chapter 3: Exploring Your Options (With Real-Life Stories!)

Now that we've set the stage with the right mindset, it's time to dive into the exciting part: figuring out how to make money from home. The great thing is, there are *so many* options—whether you want to use your skills, follow a passion, or create something entirely new.

Here, we'll explore three popular pathways: freelancing, e-commerce, and passive income. To make it even more relatable, we'll share real-life stories of people who turned their everyday talents into thriving businesses.

Freelancing: From Hobbyist to Paid Expert

Do you have a skill that people might pay for? Maybe you're good at writing, graphic design, coding, or even social media management. Whatever it is, freelancing platforms like Upwork, Fiverr, and Toptal connect you with clients looking for exactly what you offer.

Freelancing is one of the easiest ways to get started because you don't need a product or inventory—just your skills and a willingness to market yourself.

Example: Sarah's Pinterest Management Empire

Sarah was a stay-at-home mom who loved organizing Pinterest boards for fun. She'd spend hours pinning recipes, DIY projects, and inspirational quotes. One day, she stumbled upon a blog post about Pinterest marketing for small businesses and thought, *Hey, I could do that!*

She signed up for Fiverr and offered her services as a Pinterest manager. Her pitch? She could help businesses grow their audience and drive website traffic through carefully curated pins.

Within a week, Sarah landed her first client—a small boutique that needed help promoting their products. Fast-forward a few months, and Sarah was earning $5,000 a month working just 15 hours a week.

Her secret? She turned a hobby into a marketable skill and used a platform where clients were already looking for her services.

How You Can Start:

- Identify your skills: writing, editing, designing, managing social media, etc.
- Create a profile on Upwork, Fiverr, or a niche platform related to your expertise.
- Start small. Take a few gigs to build your reputation, then gradually increase your rates.

E-Commerce: How Selling Your Hobby Can Fund Your Vacation

Do you love creating things? Maybe you're into handmade crafts, art, or even baking. E-commerce platforms like Etsy, Shopify, and Amazon Handmade make it incredibly easy to sell your products to people around the world.

If physical products aren't your thing, you can sell digital products—think printable planners, templates, or recipes. And if you don't want to handle inventory at all, dropshipping on platforms like Shopify lets you sell products without ever touching them yourself.

Example: Dan's Cookie Recipe PDFs

Dan always loved baking unique cookies—think lavender lemon or chili chocolate chip. His friends and family raved about his recipes, and someone jokingly said, "You should sell these!" That comment sparked an idea.

Dan didn't want the hassle of baking and shipping cookies, so he decided to sell the recipes instead. He created simple, printable PDFs with step-by-step instructions and photos of the finished cookies. He listed them on Etsy for $5 each.

In his first month, Dan made $800. Why? Because people love unique, easy-to-follow recipes, and Dan was filling a niche.

How You Can Start:

- Pick a product: handmade crafts, vintage items, printables, or dropshipping goods.
- Use platforms like Etsy for handmade or digital goods and Shopify for more customizable stores.
- Take great photos of your products and write compelling descriptions.

Passive Income: Money While You Sleep (Literally)

The idea of passive income often sounds too good to be true — like some late-night TV ad promising millions for no work. But here's the thing: passive income is real. It's not about doing *nothing*, but about creating something once and letting it generate income over time.

Think of passive income like planting a tree: you put in the effort to grow it, but once it's mature, it keeps bearing fruit without constant attention.

Example: Tom's Investing eBook

Tom is a finance enthusiast who knows the ins and outs of basic investing. He noticed that many of his friends were intimidated by the idea of managing their money and thought, *Why not write a simple guide?*

Tom spent a weekend writing a short eBook called *Investing Basics: A Beginner's Guide to Growing Your Wealth*. He priced it at $10 and listed it on Amazon Kindle.

Here's the beauty of Tom's plan: Once the eBook was uploaded, it didn't require any additional work. Over the course of a year, Tom sold 5,000 copies, earning $50,000.

How You Can Start:

- Create a digital product like an eBook, online course, or downloadable template.

- Use platforms like Amazon Kindle, Gumroad, or Teachable to sell your product.
- Market it through social media, email lists, or blog posts.

Why These Options Work

The reason freelancing, e-commerce, and passive income are so effective is that they allow you to:

- Start with what you know. Whether it's a skill, hobby, or expertise, you already have the raw materials.
- Work at your own pace. Want to spend five hours a week or fifty? The choice is yours.
- Build something sustainable. Once you establish your systems, these income streams can grow over time.

Action Steps

1. Identify Your Strengths and Interests: Think about what you enjoy and what people often ask for your help with.
2. Choose Your Path: Start with freelancing if you have skills, e-commerce if you love creating, or passive income if you have knowledge to share.
3. Take the First Step: Sign up for a platform, create a product, or pitch your first client.

The best part? You don't have to stick to just one path. Many people start with freelancing to make quick income, then branch out into e-commerce or passive income as they gain confidence and experience.

The possibilities are endless. The only question is: which one will you start with? Let's keep going to find out!

Chapter 4: Tools You Actually Need

Working from home may sound like a breeze, but having the right tools can make or break your experience. The good news? You don't need to break the bank to get started. Whether you're freelancing, running an e-commerce store, or building passive income streams, having the right tech setup and software can save you time, reduce stress, and make your work look more professional.

The Tech Essentials for Home Success

First things first: You don't need a $2,000 MacBook Pro to start earning from home. What you *do* need is reliable equipment that gets the job done. Here's a breakdown of what you need to kick off your home-based income journey.

Budget-Friendly Starter Kit

- Laptop or Desktop Computer: Invest in a reliable laptop with decent processing power. A $500 laptop like the Lenovo Ideapad or Acer Aspire can handle most freelancing or online tasks like content writing, basic design, or video editing. *Pro Tip:* If your work involves heavy design or coding, look for models with better graphics and processing power, but don't overspend right away.

- **Microphone and Webcam:** A $40 USB microphone (like the Blue Snowball) ensures clear audio for client calls, webinars, or online teaching. Most built-in webcams work fine, but consider an upgrade like the Logitech C920 if you're creating video content.
- **Fast and Stable Internet Connection:** This is non-negotiable. No one wants a glitchy Zoom meeting! Aim for at least 50 Mbps for smooth video calls and quick uploads.

Free Tools to Save Money and Boost Productivity

There's no need to pay for fancy software when free (or nearly free) options are just as good.

Communication and Collaboration

- Zoom: Perfect for video calls with clients or teams. It's free for meetings under 40 minutes.
- Slack: Great for team communication, especially if you're working on collaborative projects.

Organization

- Google Workspace: Gmail, Google Drive, Docs, and Sheets—all in one place and free for personal use.
- Trello: A visual task manager that helps you organize your projects with drag-and-drop simplicity.

Design and Branding

- Canva: This free design tool lets you create stunning visuals for social media, eBooks, or marketing materials with zero graphic design experience.

Finance and Payments

- PayPal or Wise: Both platforms allow you to send and receive payments globally. Wise is especially useful for avoiding high currency conversion fees.

Budget Example for Getting Started

Item	Cost	Why You Need It
Laptop	$500	Reliable for all your basic work needs.
Microphone	$40	Ensures clear audio for client meetings.

Item	Cost	Why You Need It
Internet Upgrade	$50/month	Smooth Zoom calls and fast uploads/downloads.
Free Tools	$0	Zoom, Canva, Trello, and Google Workspace.
Total Investment	~$590	A one-time investment to launch your journey.

Free (or Nearly Free) Apps That Make Work Easier

1. Trello: Organize Tasks Visually

If your to-do list looks more like a jungle, Trello will be your new best friend. It's a visual project management app that lets you create boards for different projects, break them into tasks, and move them through stages (e.g., "To-Do," "In Progress," "Done").

- Use Case Example:
  Sarah, the Pinterest manager we met earlier, uses Trello to track her clients' social media schedules. Each client gets a board, and Sarah drags tasks between columns to stay on top of deadlines.

2. Calendly: Let Clients Book Meetings Without Hassle

Ever played email ping-pong trying to find the perfect time for a meeting? Calendly solves that by letting clients book directly into your calendar during your available time slots.

- Use Case Example:
  Jason, the freelance writer, uses Calendly to let potential clients schedule 15-minute consultations. It saves him hours of back-and-forth emailing every week.

3. Canva: Make Everything Look Professional

Canva is the Swiss Army knife of online tools. Need a logo, Instagram post, or eBook cover? Canva's templates make it easy — even if you have zero design skills.

- Use Case Example:
  Dan, the cookie recipe seller, uses Canva to design stunning product images and Pinterest pins that drive traffic to his Etsy shop.

4. PayPal or Wise: Get Paid from Anywhere

You'll need a way to accept payments, especially if you're working with international clients.

- PayPal is the default option for many freelancers, but Wise is a great alternative for lower transaction fees and better exchange rates.
- Use Case Example:
  Tom, the eBook author, uses PayPal to collect royalties from his book sales, while Wise helps him save money on international transactions.

Why These Tools Matter

When you're working from home, every second counts. The right tools don't just make your work easier—they save you time and keep you organized. Instead of juggling a million spreadsheets and email threads, you'll have streamlined systems in place.

Pro Tips for Tool Optimization

- Start Simple: Don't download a dozen apps you don't need. Start with essentials like Zoom, Canva, and Trello, then add as your business grows.
- Free Trials: Most premium tools offer free trials. Use them to test before committing to paid plans.

- Integrate Tools: Look for apps that work together (e.g., Google Calendar syncing with Calendly). This reduces manual work.

By investing in the right tech and learning to use free tools effectively, you'll set yourself up for long-term success without the stress of overspending. Now that you've got your tools in hand, let's move on to finding your perfect path to stress-free income in the next chapter!

Chapter 5: Finding Your Perfect Path (Without Guessing)

Let's face it—deciding how to start earning from home can feel like being in a candy store with a million options. Should you sell crafts on Etsy? Start a YouTube channel? Freelance as a writer? And what about that candle-making hobby you've always wanted to try?

It's tempting to throw spaghetti at the wall and see what sticks, but let's avoid a mess, shall we? Instead, let's use a simple, fun, and foolproof system to find your ideal path to stress-free income. Introducing... The "Skills and Thrills" Test!

The "Skills and Thrills" Test: Your Treasure Map to Success

Think of this test like building your perfect sundae. You're gathering ingredients—your skills, interests, and passions—and mixing them into something deliciously profitable. Ready? Grab a pen (or a spoon if the sundae metaphor is working for you).

Step 1: Write Down Your Skills

Imagine your friends are on a game show, and the host says, "What's [Your Name] amazing at?" What would they say? That's your starting point.

- Are you the person who can fix a Wi-Fi problem in seconds?
- Do people always ask you for help editing their resumes or essays?
- Can you create DIY party decorations that look Pinterest-perfect?

Write it all down—even the small stuff. That "weird" skill might be someone's dream service.

Step 2: Write Down Skills You Want to Learn

What have you always been curious about? Maybe it's learning how to edit videos, write a screenplay, or build websites. Add these to the list.

Think of this as your "bucket list of skills"—but instead of jumping out of airplanes, you're diving into opportunities.

Step 3: Write Down Things You Genuinely Enjoy Doing

Now comes the fun part: what do you love doing so much that you'd forget to eat lunch?

- Do you love organizing closets or color-coding your bookshelves?
- Do you get a thrill from helping friends pick out outfits?

- **Are you the person who takes 50 pictures of their coffee because the latte art is just *that* good?**

Write down your guilty pleasures, quirky hobbies, and secret talents. Nothing's off-limits.

Step 4: Find the Overlap

Here's where the magic happens. Look for the intersection between the three lists. This sweet spot is your golden ticket — a mix of what you're good at, what excites you, and what you could turn into a business or income stream.

Example: The Photography Lover

Let's say your lists look something like this:

- Skills: Taking great photos, editing pictures.
- Skills You Want to Learn: How to teach online.

- Things You Enjoy: Sharing photos and teaching friends photography tips.

Boom! You could start an online course teaching beginner photography, create a YouTube channel with tutorials, or even sell editing presets for popular photo apps like Lightroom.

Example Pathways Based on Your Interests

Here are some common interests and how you can turn them into a business (or even a mini-empire).

---

1. Love Fitness?
- Sell personalized workout plans tailored to busy moms, college students, or fitness beginners.
- Start a YouTube channel with free fitness routines and monetize through ads.

- Create a digital product like a "7-Day Home Fitness Challenge" with workout videos and meal plans.

Inspiration: Think of all those Instagram fitness coaches making six figures by posting workout clips. That could be you—except with *better* playlists.

---

2. Enjoy Gaming?
- Launch a Twitch channel where you stream gameplay with commentary (bonus points for jokes or funny reactions).
- Start a YouTube channel offering beginner guides for popular games. Offer paid coaching for people who want to level up their skills in competitive games like Fortnite or Call of Duty.

Real Talk: People are literally earning money by teaching others how to defeat video game bosses. If that's not the dream job, I don't know what is.

---

3. Can You Write?

- Ghostwrite eBooks for people too busy to write their own (and charge a premium).
- Start a blog and monetize it with ads, sponsored posts, or affiliate links.
- Create an online course teaching others how to write compelling resumes or essays.

Pro Tip: Good writers are always in demand. Whether it's blogs, scripts, or social media captions, there's a world of people who will happily pay you to put words on a page.

---

4. Obsessed with Crafts?

- Sell handmade goods on Etsy, from jewelry to hand-painted mugs.
- Teach crafting workshops via Zoom, like "How to Make a Macrame Plant Hanger."
- Create DIY kits and sell them online (complete with materials and instructions).

Fun Fact: Etsy sellers made over $2 billion in one quarter alone in 2023. Your creations could be part of that success story.

---

5. Love Cooking?
- Start a food blog featuring easy-to-make recipes with affiliate links to your favorite cookware.
- Sell digital meal plans or recipe eBooks (e.g., "10-Minute Dinners for Busy Parents").
- Host virtual cooking classes and charge per attendee.

Reality Check: The world is full of people who can burn toast. Your skills could save them from another night of sad, soggy takeout.

Why This Works

The reason this method works is simple: when you combine what you love with what you're good at, it doesn't feel like work. And when people are willing to pay for what you're offering? That's the sweet spot.

Test the Waters Before Diving In

The best part? You don't have to commit to one thing right away. Try different options to see what sticks:

- Offer a free sample of your service to a friend or neighbor and ask for feedback.
- Launch a mini product, like an eBook or guide, and see how it performs.
- Use platforms like Fiverr or Etsy to test demand without overinvesting.

The Golden Rule: Passion Meets Profit

The ultimate goal is to find something that excites you *and* pays the bills. Think of it this way: if you wouldn't mind doing it on a rainy Sunday afternoon, you're on the right track.

So, grab your list of "Skills and Thrills" and start brainstorming. Remember, every successful business starts with a single idea—and yours could be next.

In the next chapter, we'll show you how to set up your workspace, get your first clients, and start making money faster than you can say, "I love working from home!" Let's go!

Chapter 6: The Step-by-Step Playbook

Congratulations! You've reached the part where you roll up your sleeves and dive headfirst into the adventure of earning from home. You've figured out your path, built up some confidence, and now it's time to turn ideas into action.

This chapter is like your GPS—guiding you step by step to set up, launch, and grow your home-based hustle. The best part? It's not rocket science. In fact, it's a lot like baking a cake: you need the right ingredients, a solid recipe, and a pinch of patience.

Step 1: Set Up Your Home Base

Your workspace is your castle. Whether it's a corner of your living room or a dedicated office with a fancy ergonomic chair, this is the foundation of your success. The trick is creating a space that screams, "This is where the magic happens," even if it's just a small desk squeezed between your bed and the laundry basket.

What You Need for Your Castle:

- **A Dedicated Spot:** It doesn't have to be Pinterest-perfect, but it should be *yours*. Even a foldable table near a window can be transformed into a productivity zone.
- **Comfortable Seating:** Unless you enjoy walking like a robot after sitting in a bad chair all day, invest in something supportive.
- **Good Lighting:** Natural light is your best friend, but if you're working late hours, get a lamp that doesn't turn your eyes into raisins.
- **Minimal Distractions:** No TV in the background, no snacks within arm's reach (well, maybe one snack), and definitely no open tabs for online shopping.

How to Make It Fun:

Treat your workspace like a mini makeover project. Add plants, hang a motivational poster, or invest Step 1: Set Up Your Home Base

Your workspace is your castle. Whether it's a corner of your living room or a dedicated office with a fancy ergonomic chair, this is the foundation of your success. The trick is creating a space that screams, "This is where the magic happens," even if it's just a small desk squeezed between your bed and the laundry basket.

What You Need for Your Castle:

- A Dedicated Spot: It doesn't have to be Pinterest-perfect, but it should be *yours*. Even a foldable table near a window can be transformed into a productivity zone.
- Comfortable Seating: Unless you enjoy walking like a robot after sitting in a bad chair all day, invest in something supportive.
- Good Lighting: Natural light is your best friend, but if you're working late hours, get a lamp that doesn't turn your eyes into raisins.
- Minimal Distractions: No TV in the background, no snacks within arm's reach (well, maybe one snack), and definitely no open tabs for online shopping.

How to Make It Fun:

Treat your workspace like a mini makeover in quirky desk accessories. Want to feel like a CEO? Add a coffee mug that says, "World's Best Boss." (Yes, *The Office* fans, I'm talking to you.)

Why It Matters:

Imagine trying to write a client proposal while your toddler plays "drum solo" on pots and pans, the dog barks at the delivery guy, and your partner decides it's the perfect time to practice their karaoke skills. You'd lose your mind, right?

Your workspace doesn't just keep you focused—it signals to everyone in your household (including yourself) that you mean business.

Step 2: Build an Online Presence

Okay, your workspace is ready, but how do clients find you? It's simple: you need an online presence. Think of it as your digital handshake—a way for people to see who you are, what you offer, and why they should trust you.

Start Small and Mighty:

- LinkedIn: Think of LinkedIn as your online résumé but cooler. Write a short, snappy bio (skip the boring "I'm passionate about X" clichés) and highlight your skills. Bonus points for a professional profile picture—no selfies, please!
- Portfolio Website: If your work is visual (like design or photography), a simple website showcasing your projects is a game-changer. Use platforms like Wix, Squarespace, or even Canva to build a site without needing a degree in tech wizardry.
- Social Media: Depending on your niche, Instagram (for creatives), Twitter (for writers), or even TikTok (for everyone who's fun) can be great platforms to show off your work and connect with your audience.

What Your Online Presence Should Say:

1. Who You Are: Share a little personality—people love hiring real humans, not robots.
2. What You Offer: Be crystal clear about your services or products.
3. Why You're Awesome: Highlight testimonials, samples of your work, or even quirky fun facts that set you apart.

Example: Michelle's Tutoring Triumph

Michelle was a math wizard, but no one knew it outside her neighborhood. She started small—posting on LinkedIn and in a few local Facebook groups: "Hi parents! Need math help? I'm offering Zoom tutoring sessions to make math fun and easy for your kids!"

Within a week, Michelle booked her first student (her neighbor's son). Word spread like wildfire, and three months later, Michelle had 20 students and a thriving business.

Pro Tips for Building Buzz:
- Don't be afraid to share your work-in-progress online. People love following a journey.
- Post regularly, even if it's something small like a tip or a funny story related to your work.
- Interact with your audience — reply to comments, answer questions, and show genuine interest in their needs.

Step 3: Find Your First Clients

Ah, the moment you've been waiting for — your first client. This can feel like searching for a needle in a haystack, but trust me, it's more like finding Easter eggs — you just need to know where to look.

Where to Find Your Golden Clients:

1. Freelancing Platforms:

Websites like Upwork, Fiverr, and Toptal are packed with clients actively searching for help. Create a killer profile, bid on projects, and show them why you're the best choice.

2. Facebook Groups:

Join groups related to your niche or community. For example, if you're a graphic designer, look for "small business owner support" groups. Clients are often lurking in these spaces, waiting for someone to offer a solution.

3. Your Inner Circle:
   Start with friends, family, and neighbors. Let them know what you're offering—they might not need your services, but they probably know someone who does.
4. Cold Outreach (With a Twist):
   Identify potential dream clients and send them a short, friendly message. Make it personal—mention something you love about their business and explain how you can help.

Why It's Easier Than You Think:

People are *always* looking for help—they just don't know you're available yet. Once you land your first client, the momentum starts to build.

Example: Michelle's Math Empire

Michelle didn't start with a flashy website or expensive ads. She kept it simple:

1. She told her neighbors about her Zoom tutoring idea.
2. Word spread to their friends.
3. Within months, Michelle had more students than she could handle—all from starting small and showing results.

Step 4: Start Small, Then Scale

Now that you've got a few clients or sales under your belt, it's time to level up.

How to Scale Without Stress:
- Raise Your Rates: As you gain experience and build credibility, gradually increase your prices.
- Package Your Services: Offer bundles, like a three-session tutoring package or a full branding kit for new businesses.
- Add Upsells: If someone buys one service, offer them something complementary (e.g., if you design a logo, offer social media templates too).

Your First Wins Are Just the Beginning

Think of this stage as planting seeds. Each small win—whether it's a happy client, a successful project, or even a glowing testimonial—helps you grow stronger roots. Before you know it, you'll have a thriving income stream and the confidence to keep pushing further.

Your Action Plan

1. Set Up Your Space: Get your workspace ready today—even if it's just a desk and a chair.
2. Build Your Online Presence: Create a LinkedIn profile or simple portfolio.
3. Reach Out: Post in a group, email a potential client, or ask your network for referrals.
4. Celebrate Your First Win: Whether it's $5 or $500, that first income is proof that you're on the right path.

Starting your journey to stress-free earning is like building a snowball—it starts small but gains momentum as it rolls. Keep taking these steps, and soon, you'll have a full-fledged business running smoothly from the comfort of your home.

In the next chapter, we'll talk about how to grow your income streams, scale your efforts, and keep the money flowing without losing your sanity. Let's go!

Are you ready to earn?

www.ingramcontent.com/pod-product-compliance
Lightning Source LLC
Chambersburg PA
CBHW071110240526
45469CB00006BD/2415